AF226135

I prayed, GOD ANSWERED.

By Poulyana Pazand-Srouji

About the Author

When she was a teenager, Poulyana discovered her passion for writing. She wrote poetry as often as she could, as it was a way of expressing herself. Not until later, in adulthood, did she find that writing could be a form of self-healing, as she began to journal her day-to-day struggles with infertility. Through her faith, Poulyana came to understand that there was a reason why she had been chosen to experience the obstacles and tribulations involved in achieving the family she had desired for so long. Eventually, the experience opened her heart to adoption.

Poulyana was born into a family of Assyrian Christians who immigrated from the Middle East to Chicago in the late 1970s, when she was only seven months old. During her pre-teen years, Poulyana's father moved to San Jose, CA so that he could provide better opportunities for the family. Poulyana currently resides in the Bay Area, where she works as a human resources professional for a healthcare organization. However, by heart and soul, she is an avid yogi, poet, writer, reader, and adoption advocate, as well as the mother to a precious boy and a dedicated and loving daughter and wife.

This book is dedicated to my son, Noah Broneil.

You have forever changed my life.

Love, Mommy.

For years, Mommy P would stay up late at night, praying to God for a baby and hoping that, one day, God would answer her prayers. Mommy P would read the bible. Her favorite verse was 1 Samuel 1:27: "I prayed for this child, and the Lord has granted me what I asked of him". And so God gave her what her heart desired: a baby boy.

A few years passed and it was a cold, windy fall afternoon.
Mommy P and little Noah were walking through the park,
bundled up and holding hands, when little Noah stopped and
said, "Mommy, how did I come home?"

Mommy P paused and guided little Noah to a bench, where they sat down. She said, "It was the best day ever!"

Little Noah said, "Really, it was the best day?"

Mommy P nodded as she began to get teary-eyed, thinking about that special day.

"I prayed for you for years and asked God to answer my prayers," Mommy P said. "In bed at night, I would close my eyes and dream of the day when I could hold you. My favorite verse from the bible is 1 Samuel 1:27, which reads, 'I prayed for this child, and the Lord has granted me what I asked of him.'

"Everywhere I went, I would see other mommies with their children, holding hands, playing, and hugging. I longed for the day when I would get to hold you and do the same thing." Mommy P stood up. She took little Noah's hand and began to walk.

"So, when did I come?" Little Noah asked.

"It was a long time until you came. It got harder as the years went by," Mommy P said.

"Was it that hard, Mommy?"

"It was very hard but I knew that God had plans for me, so I trusted in him and remained patient. For every month that passed, it got harder, as I was waiting patiently for you. I waited and waited through every season of every year."

"Why didn't God give me to you if He knew you were waiting for so long?" Little Noah asked.

"Because He knew when the time was right to give you to me."

"Did you ever cry?"

"Yes, I did, but I trusted that God had a bigger plan for us."

"Why did God have to give you a baby?"
"Because sometimes mommies need God's help to have a baby."

"Where is my other mommy who had me?"

"God had other plans for her, so she trusted in Him that you were going to be loved. I know that she prayed that He would give you to a good family, with a mommy who would love and take care of you. God answered both of our prayers, little Noah," Mommy P said.

"So, Mommy, how did I come home?"

"God called one day and said, 'You have a beautiful baby boy and his name will be Noah.' When I brought you home, I held you in my arms with happy tears in my eyes and said, 'Welcome home, little Noah.'"

"Mommy, do you love me?"

"I love you every time I wake up in the morning and go to bed at night. I love you in between, with every breath I take and with every beat of my heart. You are my son and I am your mommy, now and forever."

Little Noah reached out with a big hug and said, "Mommy, I love you!"

All of a sudden, the wind settled and the sun began shining out from the clouds. Mommy P and little Noah looked in each other's eyes silently and knew that this was a sign from God. At that very moment, a special bond was created that would last in their hearts forever.